Soon To Be Mr & Mr

Wedding Date:

Wedding Planner

WEDDING DATE & TIME:

TO DO LIST:

VENUE ADDRESS:

BUDGET:

OFFICIANT:

WEDDING PARTY:

NOTES & REMINDERS:

Wedding Budget Planner

	TOTAL COST:	DEPOSIT:	REMAINDER:
WEDDING VENUE			
RECEPTION VENUE			
FLORIST			
OFFICIANT			
CATERER			
WEDDING CAKE			
GROOM #1 ATTIRE			
GROOM #2 ATTIRE			
JEWELRY			
BRIDESMAID ATTIRE			
GROOMSMEN ATTIRE			
HAIR & MAKE UP			
PHOTOGRAPHER			
VIDEOGRAPHER			
DJ SERVICE/ENTERTAINMENT			
INVITATIONS			
TRANSPORTATION			
WEDDING PARTY GIFTS			
RENTALS			
HONEYMOON			

12 Months Before

- [ ] SET THE DATE
- [ ] SET YOUR BUDGET
- [ ] CHOOSE YOUR THEME
- [ ] ORGANIZE ENGAGEMENT PARTY
- [ ] RESEARCH VENUES
- [ ] BOOK A WEDDING PLANNER
- [ ] RESEARCH PHOTOGRAPHERS
- [ ] RESEARCH VIDEOGRAPHERS
- [ ] RESEARCH DJ'S/ENTERTAINMENT

- [ ] CONSIDER FLORISTS
- [ ] RESEARCH CATERERS
- [ ] DECIDE ON OFFICIANT
- [ ] CREATE INITIAL GUEST LIST
- [ ] CHOOSE WEDDING PARTY
- [ ] SHOP FOR WEDDING ATTIRE
- [ ] REGISTER WITH GIFT REGISTRY
- [ ] DISCUSS HONEYMOON IDEAS
- [ ] RESEARCH WEDDING RINGS

THINGS TO REMEMBER:

9 Months Before

- FINALIZE GUEST LIST
- ORDER INVITATIONS
- PLAN YOUR RECEPTION
- BOOK PHOTOGRAPHER
- BOOK VIDEOGRAPHER
- BOOK FLORIST
- BOOK DJ/ENTERTAINMENT
- BOOK CATERER
- CHOOSE WEDDING CAKE

- CHOOSE WEDDING ATTIRE
- ORDER BRIDESMAIDS DRESSES
- RESERVE TUXEDOS
- ARRANGE TRANSPORTATION
- BOOK WEDDING VENUE
- BOOK RECEPTION VENUE
- PLAN HONEYMOON
- BOOK OFFICIANT
- BOOK ROOMS FOR GUESTS

THINGS TO REMEMBER:

6 Months Before

- ORDER THANK YOU NOTES
- REVIEW RECEPTION DETAILS
- MAKE APPT FOR TUXEDO FITTING
- CONFIRM BRIDEMAIDS DRESSES
- GET MARRIAGE LICENSE

- BOOK HAIR/MAKE UP STYLIST
- CONFIRM MUSIC SELECTIONS
- PLAN MAN SHOWER
- PLAN REHEARSAL
- SHOP FOR WEDDING RINGS

THINGS TO REMEMBER:

3 Months Before

- MAIL OUT INVITATIONS
- MEET WITH OFFICIANT
- BUY GIFTS FOR WEDDING PARTY
- BOOK FINAL FITTING
- BUY WEDDING BANDS
- PLAN YOUR HAIR STYLE
- PURCHASE SHOES
- CONFIRM PASSPORTS ARE VALID

- FINALIZE RECEPTION MENU
- PLAN REHEARSAL DINNER
- CONFIRM ALL BOOKINGS
- APPLY FOR MARRIAGE LICENSE
- CONFIRM MUSIC SELECTIONS
- DRAFT WEDDING VOWS
- CHOOSE YOUR MC
- ARRANGE AIRPORT TRANSFER

THINGS TO REMEMBER:

1 Month Before

- CONFIRM FINAL GUEST COUNT
- CONFIRM RECEPTION DETAILS
- ATTEND FINAL FITTING
- CONFIRM PHOTOGRAPHER
- WRAP WEDDING PARTY GIFTS
- CREATE PHOTOGRAPHY SHOT LIST

- REHEARSE WEDDING VOWS
- BOOK MANI-PEDI
- CONFIRM WITH FLORIST
- CONFIRM VIDEOGRAPHER
- PICK UP BRIDEMAIDS DRESSES
- CREATE WEDDING SCHEDULE

THINGS TO REMEMBER:

1 Week Before

- FINALIZE SEATING PLANS
- MAKE PAYMENTS TO VENDORS
- PACK FOR HONEYMOON
- CONFIRM HOTEL RESERVATIONS
- GIVE SCHEDULE TO PARTY
- DELIVER LICENSE TO OFFICIANT
- CONFIRM WITH BAKERY
- GIVE MUSIC LIST TO DJ
- PICK UP TUXEDOS
- AND… RELAX

THINGS TO REMEMBER:

1 Day Before

- GET MANICURE/PEDICURE
- ATTEND REHEARSAL DINNER
- GET A GOOD NIGHT'S SLEEP!
- GIVE GIFTS TO WEDDING PARTY
- FINALIZE PACKING

TO DO LIST:

The Big Day!

- [ ] GET HAIR & MAKE UP DONE
- [ ] HAVE A HEALTHY BREAKFAST
- [ ] ENJOY YOUR BIG DAY!
- [ ] MEET WITH BRIDESMAIDS
- [ ] GIVE RINGS TO BEST MAN

TO DO LIST:

Wedding Planner

ENGAGEMENT PARTY:

DATE:

TIME:

LOCATION:

NUMBER OF GUESTS:

NOTES:

MAN SHOWER:

DATE:

TIME:

LOCATION:

NUMBER OF GUESTS:

NOTES:

STAG PARTY:

DATE:

TIME:

LOCATION:

NUMBER OF GUESTS:

NOTES:

Wedding Party

MAID/MATRON OF HONOR:

PHONE: DRESS SIZE: SHOE SIZE:

EMAIL:

BRIDESMAID:

PHONE: DRESS SIZE: SHOE SIZE:

EMAIL:

BRIDESMAID #2:

PHONE: DRESS SIZE: SHOE SIZE:

EMAIL:

BRIDESMAID #3:

PHONE: DRESS SIZE: SHOE SIZE:

EMAIL:

BRIDESMAID #4:

PHONE: DRESS SIZE: SHOE SIZE:

EMAIL:

NOTES:

Wedding Party

BRIDESMAID #5:

PHONE: DRESS SIZE: SHOE SIZE:

EMAIL:

BRIDESMAID #6:

PHONE: DRESS SIZE: SHOE SIZE:

EMAIL:

BRIDESMAID #7:

PHONE: DRESS SIZE: SHOE SIZE:

EMAIL:

BRIDESMAID #8:

PHONE: DRESS SIZE: SHOE SIZE:

EMAIL:

NOTES:

Wedding Party

BEST MAN:

PHONE: WAIST SIZE: SHOE SIZE:

NECK SIZE: SLEEVE SIZE: JACKET SIZE:

EMAIL:

GROOMSMEN #1:

PHONE: WAIST SIZE: SHOE SIZE:

NECK SIZE: SLEEVE SIZE: JACKET SIZE:

EMAIL:

GROOMSMEN #2:

PHONE: WAIST SIZE: SHOE SIZE:

NECK SIZE: SLEEVE SIZE: JACKET SIZE:

EMAIL:

GROOMSMEN #3:

PHONE: WAIST SIZE: SHOE SIZE:

NECK SIZE: SLEEVE SIZE: JACKET SIZE:

EMAIL:

GROOMSMEN #4:

PHONE: WAIST SIZE: SHOE SIZE:

NECK SIZE: SLEEVE SIZE: JACKET SIZE:

EMAIL:

Wedding Party

GROOMSMEN #5:

PHONE: WAIST SIZE: SHOE SIZE:

NECK SIZE: SLEEVE SIZE: JACKET SIZE:

EMAIL:

GROOMSMEN #6:

PHONE: WAIST SIZE: SHOE SIZE:

NECK SIZE: SLEEVE SIZE: JACKET SIZE:

EMAIL:

GROOMSMEN #7:

PHONE: WAIST SIZE: SHOE SIZE:

NECK SIZE: SLEEVE SIZE: JACKET SIZE:

EMAIL:

GROOMSMEN #8:

PHONE: WAIST SIZE: SHOE SIZE:

NECK SIZE: SLEEVE SIZE: JACKET SIZE:

EMAIL:

Photographer

PHOTOGRAPHER:

PHONE:					COMPANY:

EMAIL:					ADDRESS:

WEDDING PACKAGE OVERVIEW:

EST PRICE:

INCLUSIONS:		YES ✓		NO ✓		COST:

ENGAGEMENT SHOOT:

PHOTO ALBUMS:

FRAMES:

PROOFS INCLUDED:

NEGATIVES INCLUDED:

TOTAL COST:

Videographer

VIDEOGRAPHER:

PHONE: COMPANY:

EMAIL: ADDRESS:

WEDDING PACKAGE OVERVIEW:

EST PRICE:

INCLUSIONS: YES ✓   NO ✓   COST:

DUPLICATES/COPIES:

PHOTO MONTAGE:

MUSIC ADDED:

EDITING:

TOTAL COST:

NOTES:

DJ/Entertainment

DJ/LIVE BAND/ENTERTAINMENT:

PHONE: COMPANY:

EMAIL: ADDRESS:

START TIME: END TIME:

ENTERTAINMENT SERVICE OVERVIEW:

EST PRICE:

INCLUSIONS: YES ✓   NO ✓   COST:

SOUND EQUIPMENT:

LIGHTING:

SPECIAL EFFECTS:

GRATUITIES

TOTAL COST:

NOTES:

Florist

FLORIST:

PHONE: COMPANY:

EMAIL: ADDRESS:

FLORAL PACKAGE:

EST PRICE: _____

INCLUSIONS:	YES ✓	NO ✓	COST:
GROOM BOUQUET:			
THROW AWAY BOUQUET:			
CORSAGES:			
CEREMONY FLOWERS			
CENTERPIECES			
CAKE TOPPER			
BOUTONNIERE			

TOTAL COST:

Wedding Cake/Baker

PHONE: COMPANY:

EMAIL: ADDRESS:

WEDDING CAKE PACKAGE:

COST: _____ FREE TASTING: _____ DELIVERY FEE: _____

FLAVOR:

FILLING:

SIZE:

SHAPE:

COLOR:

EXTRAS:

TOTAL COST:

NOTES:

Transportation Planner

TO CEREMONY: PICK UP TIME: PICK UP LOCATION:

GROOM #1:

GROOM #2:

GROOM'S #1 PARENTS:

GROOM'S #2 PARENTS:

BRIDESMAIDS:

GROOMSMEN:

NOTES:

TO RECEPTION: PICK UP TIME: PICK UP LOCATION:

GROOMS:

GROOM #1 PARENTS:

GROOM #2 PARENTS:

BRIDESMAIDS:

GROOMSMEN:

Wedding Planner

BACHELORE PARTY #1:

DATE: _____ LOCATION: _____

TIME: _____ NUMBER OF GUESTS: _____

NOTES:

BACHELOR PARTY #2:

DATE: _____ LOCATION: _____

TIME: _____ NUMBER OF GUESTS: _____

NOTES:

CEREMONY REHEARSAL:

DATE: _____ LOCATION: _____

TIME: _____ NUMBER OF GUESTS: _____

NOTES:

Wedding Planner

REHEARSAL DINNER:

DATE:

LOCATION:

TIME:

NUMBER OF GUESTS:

NOTES:

RECEPTION:

DATE:

LOCATION:

TIME:

NUMBER OF GUESTS:

NOTES:

REMINDERS:

Names & Addresses

CEREMONY:

PHONE: CONTACT NAME:

EMAIL: ADDRESS:

RECEPTION:

PHONE: CONTACT NAME:

EMAIL: ADDRESS:

OFFICIANT:

PHONE: CONTACT NAME:

EMAIL: ADDRESS:

WEDDING PLANNER:

PHONE: CONTACT NAME:

EMAIL: ADDRESS:

CATERER:

PHONE: CONTACT NAME:

EMAIL: ADDRESS:

FLORIST:

PHONE: CONTACT NAME:

EMAIL: ADDRESS:

Names & Addresses

BAKERY:

PHONE: CONTACT NAME:

EMAIL: ADDRESS:

SHOP:

PHONE: CONTACT NAME:

EMAIL: ADDRESS:

PHOTOGRAPHER:

PHONE: CONTACT NAME:

EMAIL: ADDRESS:

VIDEOGRAPHER:

PHONE: CONTACT NAME:

EMAIL: ADDRESS:

DJ/ENTERTAINMENT:

PHONE: CONTACT NAME:

EMAIL: ADDRESS:

HAIR/NAIL SALON:

PHONE: CONTACT NAME:

EMAIL: ADDRESS:

Names & Addresses

MAKE UP ARTIST:

PHONE: CONTACT NAME:

EMAIL: ADDRESS:

RENTALS:

PHONE: CONTACT NAME:

EMAIL: ADDRESS:

HONEYMOON RESORT/HOTEL:

PHONE: CONTACT NAME:

EMAIL: ADDRESS:

TRANSPORTATION SERVICE:

PHONE: CONTACT NAME:

EMAIL: ADDRESS:

NOTES:

Caterer Details

CONTACT INFORMATION:

PHONE: CONTACT NAME:

EMAIL: ADDRESS:

MENU CHOICE #1:

MENU CHOICE #2:

	YES ✓	NO ✓	COST:
BAR INCLUDED:			
CORKAGE FEE:			
HORS D'OEUVRES:			
TAXES INCLUDED:			
GRATUITIES INCLUDED:			

Menu Planner

HORS D'OEUVRES

1st COURSE:

2nd COURSE:

3rd COURSE:

4th COURSE:

DESSERT:

Menu Planner

HORS D'OEUVRES

1st COURSE:

2nd COURSE:

3rd COURSE:

4th COURSE:

DESSERT:

1 Week Before

	THINGS TO DO:	NOTES:
MONDAY		
TUESDAY		
WEDNESDAY		
THURSDAY		

REMINDERS & NOTES:

1 Week Before

	THINGS TO DO:	NOTES:
FRIDAY		
SATURDAY		
SUNDAY		

LEFT TO DO:

REMINDERS:

NOTES:

Wedding Guest List

NAME:	ADDRESS:	# IN PARTY:	RSVP:

Wedding Guest List

NAME:	ADDRESS:	# IN PARTY:	RSVP:

Wedding Guest List

NAME:	ADDRESS:	# IN PARTY:	RSVP:

Wedding Guest List

NAME:	ADDRESS:	# IN PARTY:	RSVP:

Wedding Guest List

NAME:	ADDRESS:	# IN PARTY:	RSVP:

Wedding Guest List

NAME:	ADDRESS:	# IN PARTY:	RSVP:

Wedding Guest List

NAME:	ADDRESS:	# IN PARTY:	RSVP:

Wedding Guest List

NAME:	ADDRESS:	# IN PARTY:	RSVP:

Wedding Guest List

NAME:	ADDRESS:	# IN PARTY:	RSVP:

Wedding Guest List

NAME:	ADDRESS:	# IN PARTY:	RSVP:

Wedding Guest List

NAME:	ADDRESS:	# IN PARTY:	RSVP:

Wedding Guest List

NAME:	ADDRESS:	# IN PARTY:	RSVP:

Wedding Guest List

NAME:	ADDRESS:	# IN PARTY:	RSVP:

Wedding Guest List

NAME:	ADDRESS:	# IN PARTY:	RSVP:

Wedding Guest List

NAME:	ADDRESS:	# IN PARTY:	RSVP:

Wedding Guest List

NAME:	ADDRESS:	# IN PARTY:	RSVP:

Wedding Guest List

NAME:	ADDRESS:	# IN PARTY:	RSVP:

Wedding Guest List

NAME:	ADDRESS:	# IN PARTY:	RSVP:

Wedding Guest List

NAME:	ADDRESS:	# IN PARTY:	RSVP:

Wedding Guest List

NAME:	ADDRESS:	# IN PARTY:	RSVP:

Wedding Guest List

NAME:	ADDRESS:	# IN PARTY:	RSVP:

Seating Chart Planner

Table #

Table #

Table #

Table #

SEATING PLANNER NOTES:

Seating Chart Planner

Table #

Table #

Table #

Table #

SEATING PLANNER NOTES:

Seating Chart Planner

Table #

Table #

Table #

Table #

SEATING PLANNER NOTES:

Seating Chart Planner

Table #

Table #

Table #

Table #

SEATING PLANNER NOTES:

Seating Chart Planner

Table #

Table #

Table #

Table #

SEATING PLANNER NOTES:

Seating Chart Planner

Table #

Table #

Table #

Table #

SEATING PLANNER NOTES:

Seating Chart Planner

Table #

Table #

Table #

Table #

SEATING PLANNER NOTES:

Seating Chart Planner

Table #

Table #

Table #

Table #

SEATING PLANNER NOTES:

Seating Chart Planner

Table #

Table #

Table #

Table #

SEATING PLANNER NOTES:

Seating Chart Planner

Table #

Table #

Table #

Table #

SEATING PLANNER NOTES:

Seating Chart Planner

Table #

Table #

Table #

Table #

SEATING PLANNER NOTES:

Seating Chart Planner

Table #

Table #

Table #

Table #

SEATING PLANNER NOTES:

Seating Chart Planner

Table #

Table #

Table #

Table #

SEATING PLANNER NOTES:

Seating Chart Planner

Table #

Table #

Table #

Table #

SEATING PLANNER NOTES:

Seating Chart Planner

Table #

Table #

Table #

Table #

SEATING PLANNER NOTES:

Seating Chart Planner

Table #

Table #

Table #

Table #

SEATING PLANNER NOTES:

Seating Chart Planner

Table #

Table #

Table #

Table #

SEATING PLANNER NOTES:

Seating Chart Planner

Table #

Table #

Table #

Table #

SEATING PLANNER NOTES:

Seating Chart Planner

Table #

Table #

Table #

Table #

SEATING PLANNER NOTES:

Seating Chart Planner

Table #

Table #

Table #

Table #

SEATING PLANNER NOTES:

Seating Chart Planner

Table #

Table #

Table #

Table #

SEATING PLANNER NOTES:

Seating Chart Planner

Table #

Table #

Table #

Table #

SEATING PLANNER NOTES:

Notes

Notes

Notes

Notes

Printed in Poland
by Amazon Fulfillment
Poland Sp. z o.o., Wrocław